IMAGES
of Sport

NORTHAMPTON TOWN
FOOTBALL CLUB

Jubilant Northampton Town players mark their promotion to the First Division with champagne in April 1965.

IMAGES
of Sport

NORTHAMPTON TOWN
FOOTBALL CLUB

Compiled by
David Walden and John Watson

TEMPUS

Tempus Publishing Limited
The Mill, Brimscombe Port,
Stroud, Gloucestershire, GL5 2QG

ISBN 0 7524 1671 5

Typesetting and origination by
Tempus Publishing Limited
Printed in Great Britain by
Midway Clark Printing, Wiltshire

Also available from Tempus Publishing

Birmingham City FC	Tony Matthews	0 7524 1862 9
Bristol City FC	Tom Hopegood/David Woods	0 7524 2040 2
Bristol Rovers FC	Mike Jay	0 7524 1150 0
Final Tie	Norman Shiel	0 7524 1669 3
The Football Programme	John Litster	0 7524 1855 6
Forever England	Mark Shaoul/Tony Williamson	0 7524 2042 9
Leeds United FC	David Saffer/Howard Dapin	0 7524 1642 1
Leeds United in Europe	David Saffer/Howard Dapin	0 7524 2043 7
Oxford United FC	Jon Murray	0 7524 1183 7
Plymouth Argyle FC	Gordon Sparks	0 7524 1185 3
Reading FC: 1871-1997	David Downs	0 7524 1061 X
Stoke City FC	Tony Matthews	0 7524 1698 7
Tottenham Hotspur FC	Roy Brazier	0 7524 2044 5
Voices of '66	Norman Shiel	0 7524 2045 3
Bristol RFC	Mark Hoskins/Dave Fox	0 7524 1875 0
Cardiff RFC	Duncan Gardiner/Alan Evans	0 7524 1608 1
The Five Nations Story	David Hands	0 7524 1851 3

Contents

Acknowledgements

The authors could not have contemplated the publication of this book without help from other sources and would like to record their thanks to the many supporters who lent their enthusiasm for the project.

Special mention must be made of Andy Roberts (*Northampton Chronicle & Echo*), Ian Davidson (*Kettering Evening Telegraph*) and *Northampton Herald & Post*, each of whom lent some splendid press photographs. Others who came to our aid with the loan of pictures were Pete Norton, Bob Thomas/Popperfoto, Stuart Robertson, Alan Burman, Rowland Jordan, Ralph Sheridan, Ray Holdsworth and Tony Ansell.

To Frank Grande, a thank you for being ever willing to check a statistical query and to James Howarth at Tempus Publishing for his supervision since our idea started to materialise in 1998.

Lastly, but certainly not least, our thanks to Shirley Watson for her support and patience at having to listen to the constant tapping and printing of the word processor over these past months.

Introduction

Sometime, around 1944, we were both introduced to the County Ground at Northampton, to witness a team clad in claret and white hooped shirts representing the local football club. The war might have given a distorted view, with many guest players appearing, but this did not dampen our enthusiasm. From that year onwards, there has only been one club for us – Northampton Town.

For several years we have nurtured the idea of producing a pictorial history of the club and to share with other supporters, both young and old, some of the memorabilia that has been collected. It also gives an opportunity to give prominence to the photographers of years gone by, whose work has helped to contribute to the social history of this part of the county of Northamptonshire. We are grateful to Tempus Publishing for bringing our plans to fruition.

One of the objectives of this book has been to portray as many past players as possible, not only those who achieved stardom, but the not so well known, some of whom played only one match, or were in the reserves. These players, as well as previous managers and officials, are all part of the ups and downs of a club that has now been in existence for over 100 years.

Most of the pictures used are focused around the County Ground, which was in use until the 1994 move to the new Sixfields Stadium. Modern technology will, no doubt, be able to provide a more extensive coverage for pictorial records in the future. Hopefully, it will observe many successful seasons for the club and its supporters in the twenty-first century.

David Walden and John Watson
June 2000

The temporary stand provides the background for Northampton Town's Ray Warburton (far left) and Chester City's Chris Lightfoot as they line-up with match officials on 30 April 1994 for one of the few remaining matches to be played at the County Ground before the move to Sixfields Stadium. Also pictured is Albert Facer, who last appeared as a professional for the Cobblers in the Third Division (South) during the 1923/24 season.

One
The Chapman Era
1897-1914

Against the background of the cricket pavilion at the County Ground, Northampton Town's players and officials of 1897/98 are portrayed in readiness for the first season in the Northamptonshire League. From left to right, back row: B. Smith, W. Westmorland, A.J. Darnell, J. Whiting, J. Sargent, G. Gyde, A. Jones. Middle row: T. Minney, M. Jones, F. Howard, F. Warner, A. Dunkley. Front row: G. Baker, C. Remmett, J. Litchfield. The committee members shown in the picture were representatives at the meeting held on 6 March 1897 at the Princess Royal Inn, Wellingborough Road, when the club was formed. The first match resulted in a 2-0 defeat at Desborough, with the third game, at home to Rushden reserves, providing the first victory by 3 goals to 1. The most impressive player, Frank Howard, was transferred to Derby County in July 1899 for £50, a much-needed fee for the club's finances.

After becoming champions of the Northamptonshire League in 1898/99, the club spent two successful years in the Midland League, before joining Kettering Town and Wellingborough Town in the Southern League in 1901/02. The 1902/03 team (shown above) finished eighth out of sixteen teams, a satisfactory start considering the strength of the opposition, which included Portsmouth, Tottenham Hotspur and West Ham United. From left to right, back row: J. Loakes (trainer), J. Bennett, F. Cook, P. Durber, R. Howe, A. Jones (secretary). Front row: J. Frost, F. Crump, A. Murrell, H. Dainty, L. Benbow, H. Brown, T. Dilks. The leading goalscorer was Len Benbow with 22 goals. He had been a member of the Nottingham Forest team that won the FA Cup in 1898.

Henry Brown, a promising local player, was transferred to West Bromwich Albion in 1903/04, as the financial needs of the club were of the most importance. Brown later became a publican but, suffering from diabetes, he had a premature death in 1934.

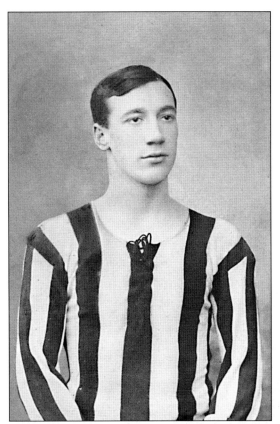

The line-up of the team for the 1904/05 season. From left to right, back row: Loakes (trainer), Neal, Bouillimer, L. Bullimer, Durber, Chapman, Howe. Front row: Clarke, Chadwick, Smith, Perkins, Benbow, G. Brown, Marriott. The name of Herbert Chapman was of great significance as it would herald a new chapter in the history of the game.

April 1907 marked a turning point in the history of Northampton Town, as this month saw the return of Herbert Chapman to the club. Within two years he led the team to the Southern League Championship, establishing himself as an outstanding football manager.

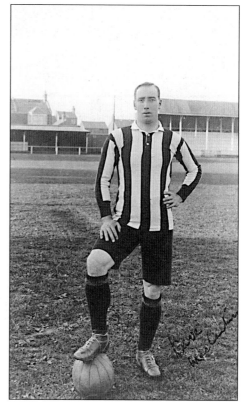

David McCartney joined the Cobblers from Chelsea in 1907, making 106 League appearances before retiring in 1910. The original stand at the Abington Avenue side of the County Ground can be clearly seen in the background.

Edwin Lloyd-Davies was transferred from Stoke City in 1907. He completed 311 appearances in the Southern League, finally retiring in 1920 when over forty years of age. Davies received 16 Welsh international caps, which included 12 during his service with Northampton. This original postcard shows the little developed Spion Kop End of the ground.

Fred Lessons scored 75 League goals for the Cobblers in 234 matches between 1907 and 1915, of which 23 were obtained during the 1908/09 Championship win. He later undertook the management of the club from 1913 to 1915.

Northampton-born Ned Freeman gave loyal service to the club from 1905 through to the first season in the Football League, his final appearance being at Swindon in March 1921. He also played for Northamptonshire County Cricket Club.

'Jock' Manning arrived at the County Ground in 1908, becoming a regular in the first team. He made 264 League appearances and scored 8 goals before retiring in 1920.

The 1908/09 champions face the camera at the Hotel End of the County Ground. From left to right, back row: R. Brittain, W. Bailiff, R. Bonthron, G. Cooch, E. Lloyd-Davies. Middle row: A. Burrows (assistant trainer), H. Foyle (financial secretary), J. Manning, W. Hickleton, D. McCartney, A. Rawlings, A. Murrell (trainer), H. Chapman (manager). Front row: C. Gyde (treasurer), G. Badenoch, R. Walker, E. Freeman, G. Lessons, A. Lewis, F. McDiarmid, F. Kilsby, A. Jones (secretary).

Albert 'Spider' Lewis led the goalscorers in 1908/09 with 30 League goals. Altogether he recorded 85 goals in 164 matches during his career with the Cobblers. He died in 1923, aged thirty-nine.

In addition to the first team winning the Southern League title, the reserves also won some trophies around 1909. From left to right, back row: A. Jones (secretary), W. Newman, A. Rawlings, R. Haywood, C. Henley, T. Evans, H. Foyle (financial secretary), A. Burrows (trainer). Front row: A. Wykes, H. Ellis, F. Walden, A. Masters, B. Tebbutt, F. Norman, J. Sutton, L. Allen. Haywood, Walden and Ellis were all on the staff of Northamptonshire County Cricket Club.

An extract from the programme for the FA Charity Shield match staged at Chelsea's ground on 28 April 1909 (right). The Football League champions of 1908/09, Newcastle United, won 2-0. The table for the Southern League (below) shows the impressive record the Cobblers attained.

NEWCASTLE UNITED v. NORTHAMPTON.

FOOTBALL ASSOCIATION CHARITY SHIELD MATCH.

WEDNESDAY, APRIL 28th, 1909.   Kick-off 5.0 p.m.

NEWCASTLE UNITED (Black and White Stripes).

1
LAWRENCE
Goal

2
McCRACKEN
Right Back

3
WHITSON
Left Back

4
HOWIE
Right Half

5
VEITCH
Centre Half

6
McWILLIAM
Left Half

7
RUTHERFORD
Outside Right

8
HIGGINS
Inside Right

9
ALLAN
Centre

10
WILSON
Inside Left

11
ANDERSON
Outside Left

12
FREEMAN
Outside Left

13
LEWIS
Inside Left

14
LESSONS
Centre

15
WALKER
Inside Right

16
McDIARMID
Outside Right

17
F. DUNKLEY
Left Half

18
McCARTNEY
Centre Half

19
MANNINC
Right Half

20
DAVIES
Left Back

22
COOCH
Goal

21
BONTHRON
Right Back

NORTHAMPTON (Claret and White Stripes).

Referee - - - Mr. J. R. SCHUMACHER.

ANY ALTERATIONS WILL BE NOTIFIED ON THE BOARD.

Printed and Published for the Proprietors (The Chelsea Football and Athletic Co., Ltd.), by Jas. Truscott & Son, Ltd., London.

SOUTHERN LEAGUE.
DIVISION 1.   Goals.

	Plyd.	Won	Lost	Drn.	For	Agst.	Pts.
Northampton	40	25	10	5	90	45	55
Swindon Town	40	22	13	5	96	55	49
Southampton	40	19	11	10	67	58	48
Portsmouth	40	18	12	10	68	60	46
Bristol Rovers	40	17	14	9	60	63	43
Exeter City	40	18	16	6	56	65	42
New Brompton	39	17	16	6	48	59	40
Reading	40	11	11	18	60	57	40
Luton	40	17	17	6	59	60	40
Plymouth Argyle	40	15	15	10	46	47	40
Millwall Athletic	40	16	18	6	59	61	38
Southend United	39	14	16	9	52	54	37
Watford	40	14	17	9	51	64	37
Leyton	39	14	17	8	51	55	36
Crystal Palace	40	12	16	12	62	62	36
West Ham United	40	16	20	4	56	60	36
Queen's Park Rangers	38	12	15	11	52	49	35
Brighton and Hove Albion	40	14	19	7	60	61	35
Norwich City	39	12	17	10	59	75	34
Coventry City	40	15	21	4	64	91	34
Brentford	40	13	20	7	58	73	33

17

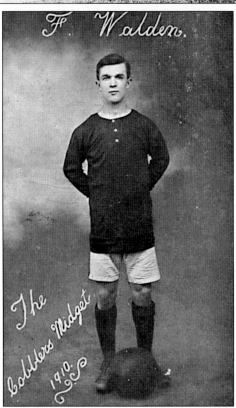

The team for 1909/10 proudly display the handsome Southern League shield. They went on to finish in fourth place, with 90 goals scored, which was another good performance. Lewis again topped the goalscorers list with 26. A debut hat-trick for 'Fanny' Walden in a 6-1 victory over Luton Town at the County Ground marked the beginning of an outstanding career. From left to right, back row: F. Whittaker, R. Bonthron, T. Thorpe, E. Lloyd-Davies. Middle row: A. Burrows (assistant trainer), C. Gyde, J. Manning, D. McCartney, F. Dunkley, R. Codling, R. Brittain, H. Foyle (financial secretary), A. Murrell (trainer). Front row: H. Chapman (manager), F. McDiarmid, R. Walker, G. Lessons, A. Lewis, E. Freeman, W. Beadling, A. Jones (secretary).

Frederick 'Fanny' Walden was born in Wellingborough in 1888. An outstanding footballer for Northampton Town, Tottenham Hotspur and England, he also made 258 appearances for Northamptonshire in first-class cricket and became a county legend in his own lifetime.

George Badenoch signed for the Cobblers in 1907, stayed for two seasons and usually occupied the number seven shirt. He became a war casualty in 1915.

PROMINENT FOOTBALLERS.

G. BADENOCH,

NORTHAMPTON.

PROMINENT FOOTBALLERS.

R. P. BONTHRON,

NORTHAMPTON.

Scottish-born Robert Bonthron joined the club in 1908 and also remained for two seasons before transferring to Birmingham.

PROMINENT FOOTBALLERS.

R. C. BRITTAIN.

NORTHAMPTON.

Signed from Portsmouth in 1907, Richard Brittain made 13 appearances in Herbert Chapman's championship team in 1908/09.

PROMINENT FOOTBALLERS.

G. COOCH,

NORTHAMPTON.

Wellingborough-born George Cooch missed only two matches as goalkeeper in 1908/09. Originally signed from Kettering Town, he later spent several seasons after the First World War as trainer to Aston Villa.

Defender William Hickleton transferred from Portsmouth to Northampton Town in 1907 and, although he stayed for two years, did not retain a regular place in the team. Moving further north, he later joined Coventry City.

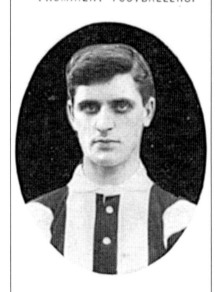

W. R. HICKLETON.

NORTHAMPTON.

F. KILSBY.

NORTHAMPTON.

Frank Kilsby, born at Fenny Stratford, played in only six matches for the Cobblers, but obtained recognition by being included in a set of cigarette cards issued in 1907.

PROMINENT FOOTBALLERS.

F. McDIARMID.

NORTHAMPTON.

For four seasons, from 1907/08 to 1910/11, Fred McDiarmid played an important role for the team, both as a winger and in defence. He missed only one match in the 1908/09 championship season.

Third position was attained by this team of 1911/12, with Harry King, signed from Central League side Crewe Alexandra, heading the scoring list together with Fred Lessons, both netting 19 goals. Later, Bradshaw and King were to play for Arsenal, both being included in the team that represented the London club's last appearance in the Second Division in 1915. From left to right, back row: Murrell (trainer), Smith, Manning, Lewis, Thorpe, Lessons, Brittan, Clipston, Burrows (assistant trainer). Front row: Walden, Bradshaw, Whittaker, Lloyd-Davies, King, Hampson, Freeman.

The 1912/13 team finished in mid-table, but suffered a 7-2 FA Cup defeat at the hands of Blackburn Rovers. From left to right, back row: W. Tull, F. Clipstone, E. Lloyd-Davies, R. Hughes. Middle row: J. Manning, B. Tebbutt, J. Hampson, A. Rawlings, E. Tomkins, A. Burrows (trainer). Front row: W. Bull (manager), H. Redhead, F. Walden, H. King, F. Lessons, A. Lewis, C. Smith, E. Freeman, A. Jones (secretary). Inset: T. Thorpe. Walter Tull, signed from Tottenham Hotspur, was Northampton Town's first coloured player. He was later killed in action in 1915.

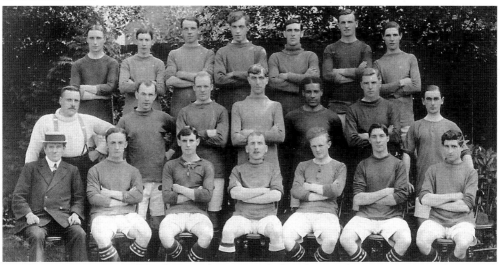

Northampton Town's staff for the 1914/15 season, before the Southern League ceased activities for the duration of the war. From left to right, back row: C. Smith, Barrett, Tomblin, H. Smith, Thorpe, Langham, Whitworth. Middle row: Burrows (trainer), Manning, Lessons, York, Tull, Clipstone, Tomkins. Front row: A. Jones (secretary), Freeman, Dawson, Lloyd-Davies, Lockett, Bellamy, Hughes. Bellamy was later to become a prominent player for Northamptonshire in first-class cricket during the 1920s and '30s.

Geddington-born Fred Clipstone signed from Portsmouth in 1910 and stayed with the club until 1920, when he retired from football. He died soon after leaving the game as a result of illness brought about whilst on active service during the First World War.

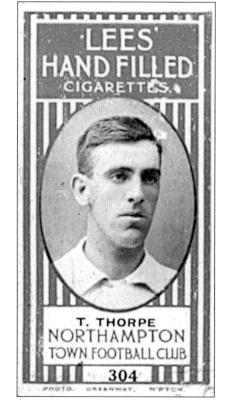

Tommy Thorpe, a goalkeeper, joined the club from Barnsley in 1909 and stayed to play in the club's first season in the Football League, 1920/21. He also played first-class cricket for Northamptonshire.

Bryan Tebbutt, from Northampton, made just 12 appearances, but was included in a rare set of football cigarette cards issued by J. Lees, a cigarette manufacturer based in Northampton.

Walter Bull, like Herbert Chapman, was a former Tottenham Hotspur player. He succeeded his former colleague in 1912 as the club's manager, but only stayed until the end of the year.

Appointed by Walter Bull, Harry Burrows served the club in the capacity of trainer until well into the Football League days.

A familiar figure in the town was schoolteacher Arthur 'Dado' Jones, who became secretary at the formation of the club in 1897. He remained in that capacity until the formative years of the Third Division (South).

Two
Between the Wars
1920-1939

The team group from 1920/21, the first season in the Football League. From left to right, back row: A. Burrows (trainer), Watson, Jobey, Smith, Hewison, Mackechnie, A. Jones (secretary). Front row: Pease, Grendon, Whitworth, Lockett, Thomas, Tomkins, Freeman. The first match, away to Grimsby Town, resulted in a 2-0 defeat. Queens Park Rangers, at the County Ground, were the next opponents and provided the club with a first victory by 2-1, both the goals being scored by Lockett. Tomkins and Freeman also played first-class cricket for Northamptonshire.

Seventeenth position was attained in the second League season, 1921/22. No victories were achieved away from home, with an 8-0 defeat at Southampton and a 7-0 reverse at Brighton, helping to a total of 54 goals conceded on the club's travels. From left to right, back row: Williams, Jeffs, Grendon. Middle row: Burrows (trainer), Watson, Hewison, Ambidge, Jobey, Bedford. Front row: Pease, Hawtin, Seabrook, Whitworth, Lockett, Harron, Tomkins.

Arthur T. Davies made 10 appearances in 1921/22, having previously played for Cambridge University and Corinthians. He received an amateur international cap for England in 1920/21 against Wales. Davies later concentrated on a teaching career in physics at Northampton Grammar School.

Arthur Seabrook joined the club in 1921/22 and stayed three seasons without obtaining a regular first-team place. He did, however, sign off in his penultimate match for the club with a hat-trick, part of an 8-0 defeat of Southend United.

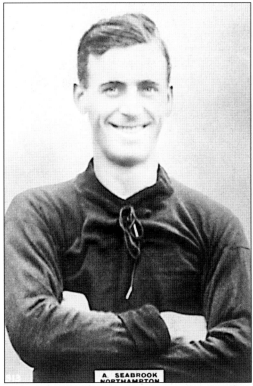

Eighth position was a much-improved season's return for the 1923/24 team. From left to right, back row: A. Burrows (trainer), F. Newton, W. Watson, H. Smith, F. Brett, E. Wood, R. Hewison (player-manager), W. Westmorland (director). Front row: C. Gyde (director), W. Pease, W. Wood, W. Lockett, C. Myers, L. Page, W. Russell Seal (director). On ground: W. Williams.

Northampton Town reserves before a match at Bournemouth during the 1923/24 season. The goalkeeper, Len Hammond (back row, fourth from left), played over 300 matches in the first team before transferring to Notts County in 1933. The result of this visit to the south coast was a 4-2 defeat.

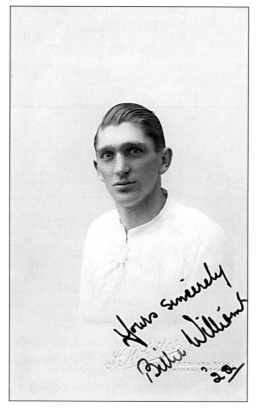

Billie Williams provided a rare instance of a player from the Cobblers being chosen for his country, when he was capped for Wales against Scotland in 1925.

During the early 1920s Northampton Town possessed two wingers of great skill. Louis Page was a favourite of the County Ground supporters and was good enough to be selected for England after transferring to Burnley.

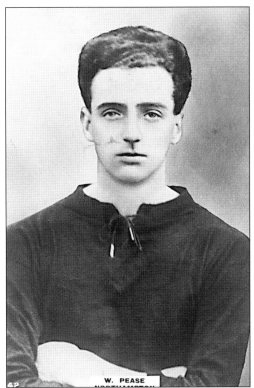

The other half of the wing combination was Billy Pease, later to be capped for England while playing for Middlesbrough. Both Page and Pease were to represent their country in 1927 against Wales.

Northampton Town F.C.
SUPPORTERS' CLUB

BAZAAR

TOWN HALL, NORTHAMPTON
September 16, 17 & 18, 1926

At the close of the 1926/27 season the assets of the club were exceeded by liabilities of £1,500. As this was a heavy millstone to carry, the Supporters' Club arranged for a bazaar to be held over three days at the Town Hall. It was hoped that some of the money raised would be allocated for terracing on the Spion Kop.

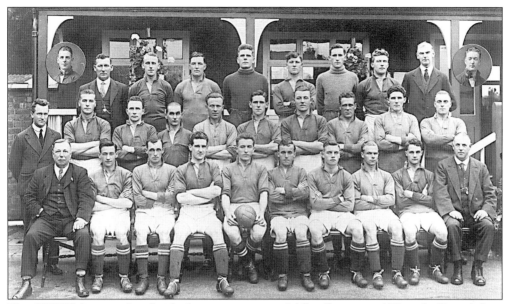

The 1927/28 line-up that finished as runners-up to Millwall, scoring 102 goals. From left to right, back row: J. Webster (trainer), Jeffs, Watson, Hammond, Russell, Cave, Allon, Newman (assistant trainer). Middle row: J. Tresadern (manager), Wilson, Daly, Tomkins, Odell, Andrews, Maloney, Hoten, Brett, Smith. Front row: T. Gillitt (director), Wells, Aitken, Price, Loasby, Shaw, Fraser, George, Taylor, W. Russell Seal (director). Insets: Cockle, Cowen.

Ralph Hoten scored five goals in the 8-1 victory against Crystal Palace at home in October 1928, a club record.

The Cobblers line-up for a match at Bournemouth in February 1930. From left to right: Russell, Loasby, Sissons, Hammond, Hoten, Smith, Maloney, Allon, A. Dawes, Weston, Brett. Bournemouth won 3-1.

The format of the matchday programme changed little between the wars. This programme is for the opening fixture of the 1931/32 season. The result was a 1-0 victory for the Cobblers, with Wells scoring the winning goal.

This 1931/32 team finished in fourteenth position in the table. From left right, back row: Scott, Bowen, Boyle, Hammond, Cave, Davies, F. Dawes. Middle row: J. English (manager), McMullen (trainer), Todd, Wonnacott, Anthony, Inglis, Berridge, Oakley, Park, Newman (assistant trainer), J. Marlow (secretary). Front row: T. Gillitt (director), Riches, Allon, Mortimer, Radford, Odell, Taylor, A. Dawes, Weston, Wells, W. Russell Seal (director).

Players and officials face the camera prior to the start of the 1933/34 season. From left to right, back row: T. Boyle, W. Thompson, F. Davies, A. Wallington, W. Cave, F. Dawes, E. Warren, J. Dowsey. Middle row: J. English (manager), W. Newman (trainer), C. Allan, A. Brown, J. McGuire, O. Park, F. McMenemy, T. Crilly, W. Inglis (assistant trainer), J. Marlow (secretary). Front row: C. Gillitt (director), J. Cherry, J. Young, W. Fraser, A. Dawes, A. Wheeler, G. Henson, D. Tolland, T. Wells, L. Riches, R.P. Seal (director).

The 1933/34 season brought a mid-table position in the League competition, but was highlighted by reaching the fifth round of the FA Cup. From left to right, back row: Dowsey, Newman (trainer), Crilly, T. Allen, C. Allen, Riches, Brown. Seated: Cherry, Boyle, Henson, A. Dawes, Wells, McGuire.

The players on parade in early 1934 before embarking on an important FA Cup game. From left to right: J. Engligh (manager), L. Riches, T. Boyle, F. Dawes, D. Tolland, J. McGuire, T. Crilly, T. Allen, A. Mitchell, G. Henson, F. Davies, T. Wells, M. Newman (trainer).

Huddersfield Town.

Goal
1 **Turner**

Backs
2 **Roughton**   3 **Mountford**

Half-Backs
4 **Willingham**   5 **Young**   6 **Campbell**

Forwards
7 **Williams**   8 **McLean**   9 **Mangnall**   10 **Luke**   11 **Bott**

 FOR BEST REPORTS

12 **Wells**   13 **Tolland**   14 **Henson**   15 **Boyle**   16 **Mitchell**

Forwards
17 **Davies**   18 **McGuire**   19 **Riches**

Half-Backs
20 **Dawes**   21 **Crilly**

Backs
22 **Allen**

Goal

Northampton Town.

Referee—E. V. GOUGH (Staffordshire)   Colours—Claret Shirts, White Knickers.
Linesmen—N. BOOTH (Red Stripe).   J. W. LEGGE (Blue Stripe).

On 27 January 1934 the Cobblers handed out a 2-0 defeat to Huddersfield Town in the fourth round of the FA Cup. This rare programme of the event shows the team line-ups. Huddersfield, third in the First Division at the time and with home advantage, were expected to progress in the competition. However, goals from Boyle and Wells provided a shock result, with a fifth round tie at Preston as the team's reward. There were to be no surprises at Preston, though, with the home side winning 4-0 in front of a crowd of over 40,000.

Left: Colleagues James McGuire (standing) and Joseph McAleer pose for a studio portrait in 1933. Their careers were to go in very different directions. McGuire established himself in the team, leaving after 70 appearances for America. Following his retirement from the game, he became president of the National American Soccer Federation and later a member of FIFA. McAleer's career took a different turn and, despite scoring 6 goals in only 8 matches, he moved to Lincoln City at the end of the 1933/34 season. *Below left:* A vastly experienced player, Tommy Boyle was recruited from Manchester United in 1930. An inside forward, he had been a member of Sheffield United's FA Cup winning team in 1925. *Below right:* Defender Alf Brown transferred from Oldham Athletic in 1933 and stayed for three seasons before moving to Mansfield Town. He is portrayed on a card from a series produced by manufacturers of $\frac{1}{2}$d bars of chewing gum, and avidly collected by schoolboys of that era.

Forward · T. BOYLE
NORTHAMPTON TOWN F.C.

CLARET JERSEYS, WHITE KNICKERS.

Back · A. BROWN
NORTHAMPTON TOWN F.C.

CLARET JERSEYS, WHITE KNICKERS.

Now under the management of Syd Puddefoot, the 1936/37 players assemble at the County Ground. From left to right, back row: Rawlings, Hinson, E. Hewitt, Thompson, S. Puddefoot (manager), Gormlie, Cave, McGuire, Cook, Thayne, Potter, H. Lea (director). Middle row: M. Newman (trainer), Hoult, Billingham, Turner, Little, Wallbanks, Blencowe, J. Hewitt, Russell, Bell, E. Hawtin (director). Front row: G. Hooton (director), Simpson, Lyman, Robson, Tolland, T. Gillitt (chairman), Mackie, Riley, Riches, O'Rourke, J. Marlow (secretary). The team completed the season in seventh position in the Third Division (South), but suffered a humiliating 6-1 defeat in the FA Cup by amateurs Walthamstow Avenue.

The 1937/38 season opened at the County Ground on 28 August with a reserve team match between the Cobblers and Portsmouth. In this photograph, the home team goalkeeper, Jack Jones, watches as Portsmouth attack the Spion Kop end of the ground. The visitors won this encounter 2-0.

March 1938 saw the debut of Fred Tilson, a former England player signed from Manchester City. He stayed until the 1938/39 season, later moving north to become trainer to York City.

Warney Cresswell was the manager of this 1938/39 team that finished a disappointing seventeenth in the final League table. From left to right, back row: M. Newman (trainer), K. McCullough, K. Gunn, W. Gormlie, S. Russell, T. Postlethwaite, A. Ford. Front row: R. King, F. Tilson, J. Haycox, J. Lauderdale, J. McCartney, W. Thayne.

Keilor McCullough, an Irishman, was one of three players who came from Manchester City to Northampton Town in exchange for the promising Maurice Dunkley. Photographic sheets of players were given away with each match programme during the 1938/39 season.

Goalkeeper Bill Gormlie arrived from Blackburn Rovers in 1935, staying until the outbreak of war in 1939. He then transferred to Lincoln City.

Northampton-born Bobby King made his debut in December 1937 at Notts County, the result of which was a 5-0 defeat. He displayed his promising talent until 1939 before signing for Wolves. He was to be one of many players whose career was cut short by war and in 1947 he returned to the County Ground.

Defender Syd Russell suffered a broken leg at Southend in April 1939. This accident resulted in his leg having to be amputated. Everton sent a strong side for a benefit match for him, with stars such as Tommy Lawton and Joe Mercer taking part.

Three
Wartime and
Guest Players

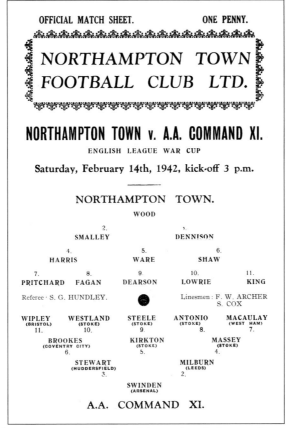

OFFICIAL MATCH SHEET.　　　ONE PENNY.

NORTHAMPTON TOWN
FOOTBALL CLUB LTD.

NORTHAMPTON TOWN v. A.A. COMMAND XI.
ENGLISH LEAGUE WAR CUP
Saturday, February 14th, 1942, kick-off 3 p.m.

NORTHAMPTON TOWN.
WOOD

2.
SMALLEY

3.
DENNISON

4.　　　　　　5.　　　　　6.
HARRIS　　　WARE　　　SHAW

7.　　　8.　　　9.　　　10.　　　11.
PRITCHARD　FAGAN　DEARSON　LOWRIE　KING

Referee · S. G. HUNDLEY.　　　　　Linesmen : F. W. ARCHER
S. COX

WIPLEY　　WESTLAND　STEELE　ANTONIO　MACAULAY
(BRISTOL)　　(STOKE)　　(STOKE)　(STOKE)　(WEST HAM)
11.　　　　10.　　　　9.　　　　8.　　　　7.

BROOKES　　　　KIRKTON　　　MASSEY
(COVENTRY CITY)　　(STOKE)　　　(STOKE)
6.　　　　　　5.　　　　　　4.

STEWART　　　　MILBURN
(HUDDERSFIELD)　　(LEEDS)
3.　　　　　　2.

SWINDEN
(ARSENAL)

A.A. COMMAND XI.

The one-page match programme that the club produced during the war years. This 1942
AA Command XI shows the quality of the players witnessed on the County Ground during
those desperate days, giving short breaks from the war effort.

Northampton Town, 1944/45. These were the players that represented the club on the opening day of the season at home against West Bromwich Albion, who defeated the Cobblers 4-1. From left to right, back row: T. Smith (manager), J. Jennings (trainer), unknown, Perry, Lee, Cransfield, Cooper, Pritchard, Newman (assistant trainer). Middle row: Roberts, Harris, Smalley, James, Hurrell. Front row: Coley, Welsh, Stephens.

The transitional season of 1945/46 gave many managers the time to rebuild their teams in readiness for the resumption of the Football League programme after the war.
Northampton Town manager, Tom Smith, took this opportunity to sign Harry Lowery, an experienced wing-half from West Bromwich Albion. The tall, blond-haired player made 76 League appearances before leaving the club at the end of the 1948/49 season.

The 1945/46 season was a transitional one with clubs still able to recruit guest players. Northampton took part in the Third Division South (North Region) League and the Third Division South Cup. No fewer than 41 players are listed as having appeared in these competitions for Northampton. Those shown here are, from left to right, back row: J. Jennings (trainer), Jones, Wallington, Shepherdson, Neal, Lee, Welsh, Ellwood, M. Newman (assistant trainer), T. Smith (manager). Middle row: Wilson, Roberts, Dennison, Barron, Smalley. Front row: J. Dixon, Morrall.

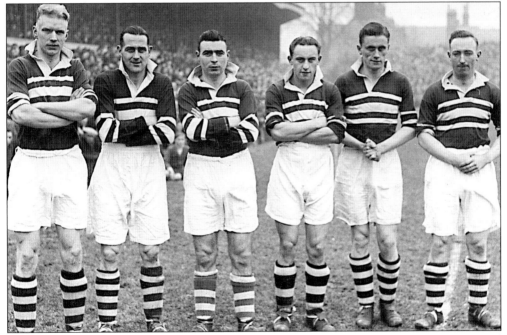

In 1945/46 the FA Cup was contested on a home and away basis. After defeating Chelmsford City and Notts County, the Cobblers were drawn against Millwall in the third round. Pictured in front of a large crowd are: Lowery, Sankey, Blunt, Fowler, Hughes, Yarker. The home fixture resulted in a 2-2 draw, with Millwall winning 2-0 in the second leg. Blunt and Hughes were the scorers at Northampton.

W. Barron, R. Jones and D. Smith are pictured before a match in the 1945/46 season. April 1946 saw Bill Barron cross to the cricket side of the ground and to establish himself as a regular player for Northamptonshire County Cricket Club. Before the war he had played for Durham in the Minor Counties Championship and in 1945 he made a single first-class appearance for Lancashire.

Four

Back to Real Football at Last

1946-1960

The 1946/47 set of players photographed before the traditional August trial match. Hopes were high that the season would realise the long-standing ambition of achieving promotion for the first time. From left to right, back row: D. Littlemore, M. Newman (assistant trainer), M. Collings, T. Smalley, T. Smith (manager), R. Dennison, D. Steers, J. Jones, J. Jennings (trainer), D. Scott, A. MacGregor, R. Dixon, S. Stanton, J. Pyle, R. Hilliard, R. Street. Middle row: M. McKenna, S. Heaselgrave, R. Jenkins, G. Roberts, J. Sankey, E. Blunt, L. White, S. Baines, A. Morrall. Front row: D. Smith, K. Baucutt, G. Skelton, J. Strathie, W. Jennings, R. Allen, G. Neal.

The reserves of 1946/47 line up before a sparse crowd at the County Ground. From left to right, back row: Ashley, Neal, Quinney, Scott, Strathie, MacGregor, McKenna, M. Newman (trainer), White. Middle row: Williams, Heaselgrave, Allen, Jennings. Front row: Jenkins, Baines.

A crowd of 12,013 watched the opening match of the first post-war season on 31 August 1946. Long standing rivals, Swindon Town, were defeated 4-1 with Sammy Heaselgrave and Alf Morrall each scoring two goals. This picture shows David Smith challenging the Swindon goalkeeper, supported by Sammy Heaselgrave (far left).

The Swindon goalkeeper is clearly relieved as the ball sails over the crossbar.

The traditional Christmas morning fixture always attracted a large following; this match in 1946 having an attendance of 13,501. The result was a 2-2 draw. The one-page programme for the day did not contain a single advertisement, but found enough space to record the splendid FA Cup second round second replay victory by 8-1 against local rivals Peterborough United.

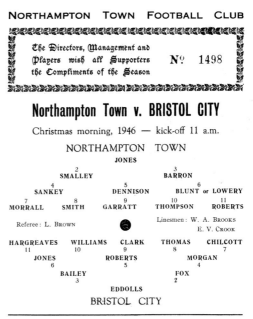

NORTHAMPTON TOWN FOOTBALL CLUB

The Directors, Management and Players wish all Supporters the Compliments of the Season   Nº 1498

Northampton Town v. BRISTOL CITY

Christmas morning, 1946 — kick-off 11 a.m.

NORTHAMPTON TOWN

JONES

2 SMALLEY   3 BARRON

4 SANKEY   5 DENNISON   6 BLUNT or LOWERY

7 MORRALL   8 SMITH   9 GARRATT   10 THOMPSON   11 ROBERTS

Referee: L. BROWN   Linesmen: W. A. BROOKS
                                        E. V. CROOK

HARGREAVES   WILLIAMS   CLARK   THOMAS   CHILCOTT
11   10   9   7

JONES   ROBERTS   MORGAN
6   5   4

BAILEY   FOX
3   2

EDDOLLS

BRISTOL CITY

Now for Preston. What a treat for the supporters who were fortunate enough to see the second re-play v. Peterborough at Coventry. Every man played great football and played as a team, but we must just mention the fact that Archie Garrett scored four goals and could have scored more if he had not been so unselfish. Without being unfair to Peterborough they were out-played and out-classed. The grand open game we played would have beaten many first-class teams.

Christmas Programme: 2d.

The FA Cup draw for the third round brought Preston North End to the County Ground, a match which attracted nearly 17,000 people. The Cobblers put up stiff opposition, with England star, Tom Finney, requiring much attention. Bill Barron (partly hidden) and Harry Lowery close in on Finney, watched by goalkeeper Dave Scott.

Preston's goalkeeper, Fairbrother, clears from Archie Garrett. Gordon Roberts scored for the Cobblers in the 2-1 defeat. This match was played on 11 January 1947, before the onset of a bitterly cold winter.

After completing his army service and having made some guest appearances during the war, David Smith's League debut for the Cobblers came in August 1946. When he retired at the end of the 1950/51 season he had played in 128 League matches, scoring 30 goals. He later served the Cobblers, both in the secretarial and managerial positions, eventually taking over in a similar capacity at Aldershot.

Archie Garrett transferred from Hearts to Northampton Town in September 1946. By the end of the 1946/47 season he had scored 26 League goals and 6 in the FA Cup. Other clubs soon became interested in him and in late 1947 he joined Birmingham City. However, his stay with Birmingham was not so successful, eventually leading to a return to the County Ground a year later. His was a comeback that brought a special welcome.

The cartoon showing the welcome given to Archie Garrett and another new signing, Tim McCoy from Portsmouth, in December 1948. This and many other such cartoons were regular features in the *Northampton Chronicle & Echo* around this time.

Above left: Welshman Gwyn Hughes, a loyal servant for the Cobblers after the war, was equally at home in defence or attack. When he left the club for Bedford Town in 1956 he had made over 200 appearances. *Above right:* The evening shadows are cast over captain Bob Dennison in August 1947 as he clears his lines against Torquay United. The kick-off time would have been at 6.30 p.m. as there were no floodlights available for a few more years. The result was a 1-0 win for the Cobblers. *Right:* In November 1947, Tommy Lawton made headline news by signing for Third Division Notts County, having previously been with Chelsea in the First Division. His first match for his new club was at Northampton and his presence attracted a crowd of 18,272. He is pictured (left) being greeted by Northampton's Bob Dennison.

A pre-match stroll by Harry Thompson, David Smith and Tom Smalley before a match at Brighton. Thompson and Smalley had previously been colleagues at Wolverhampton Wanderers in pre-war days. During his stay at Wolverhampton, Smalley was capped for England against Wales in 1936.

Players and officials line up outside the County Ground for an away trip, soon after the Second World War. From left to right: F. York (director), the coach driver, G. Roberts, A. Garrett, J. Briscoe, T. Smith (manager), F. Speakman (press representative), W. Barron, D. Scott, unknown, D. Smith, G. Hooton (director), J. Jennings (trainer), R. Dennison, H. Thompson.

A cartoon summary of the characters involved in the 1947/48 season for Northampton Town. This was a farewell year for Bob Dennison, although he was to make a welcome return as manager in 1949.

The 1948/49 season saw Tom Smith's team avoid the need for re-election by a fraction of difference in goal average over Aldershot. Before the end of the campaign Smith had left the club and been replaced by Bob Dennison. Around this period Tom Fowler was establishing his place in the team and a career that would continue until 1961, ending with a record 521 League appearances. From left to right, back row: T. Smith (manager), T. Smalley, J. Jones, D. Smith, A. Morrall, J. Jennings (trainer). Front row: W. Barron, T. Fowler, G. Roberts, R. Dennison, J. Sankey, E. Blunt, S. Heaselgrave.

The 1949/50 players and officials line up before Bob Dennison's first complete season in charge. The team finished as runners-up to Notts County. From left to right, back row: Murphy, Jeffrey, McCulloch, Collins, Woollard, Candlin, McCoy, Barron, Coley, Maxwell, D. Smith. Middle row: M. Newman (assistant trainer), Southam, Horne, Bowen, W.H. Smith, Henderson, Ansell, Hughes, Freimanis, Fisher, Clamp, J. Jennings (trainer). Front row: English, King, Mulgrew, R. Dennison (manager), P. Hutton (director), E.C. Hawtin (director), W. Penn (director), N. Wooding (director), Mitchell, Fowler, Garrett.

Tim McCoy leads his team out at the County Ground on Thursday 25 August for the first home match of the successful 1949/50 season. Until the advent of floodlights most midweek matches were played on Thursdays, as this was a half-day holiday for local shopkeepers. McCoy is followed onto the field by Candlin, Murphy and D. Smith. The result was a 4-3 victory over Newport County.

Saturday 3 September 1949 was an away fixture at Walsall and the team and officials line up before commencing the journey. From left to right: E. Hawtin (director), P. Hutton (director), R. Dennison (manager), unknown, F. York (director), T. McCoy, E. Murphy, M. Candlin, R. King, A. McCulloch, M. Dunkley, W. Coley, J. Ansell, K. Maxwell, J. Jennings (trainer), M. Newman (assistant trainer). Standing behind the team is Fred Speakman, a journalist who covered sport around Northampton for many years. The team returned from this match with a 3-1 victory – King, Murphy and Mitchell scoring the goals.

A break in training allows the 1949 squad to face the camera. From left to right: Murphy, Dixon, Mitchell, McCulloch, Candlin, Garrett, Hughes, Freimanis, Coley, McCoy, Ansell.

Gymnasium work for members of Dennison's 1949 team. From left to right: Mitchell, Candlin, Murphy, Dixon. Arthur Dixon's arrival from Hearts during mid-season made an immediate impact and proved to be an inspired signing. His ability was noted by other clubs and in 1951 he joined Leicester City, later finishing his career with Kettering Town.

Notts County's Tommy Lawton directs a header at the Northampton goal at Meadow Lane in April 1950. Ben Collins and Maurice Candlin watch with concern in this match won 2-0 by County. Just two days later, in muddy and wet conditions, the Cobblers gained some revenge by recording a resounding 5-1 victory at the County Ground.

During the 1949/50 season the FA Cup provided much interest, with the Cobblers reaching the fifth round. Victories over Walthamstow Avenue and Torquay United in the first and second rounds brought Southampton to the County Ground in January 1950. The result at home brought a 1-1 draw, followed by a handsome 3-2 win at The Dell in a midweek replay. Northampton's Maurice Candlin greets Southampton's Eric Webber before the kick-off in the home tie, watched by a crowd of 23,209.

The next round brought an away draw at Bournemouth, the result ending 1-1. The replay, with an attendance of over 22,000, was an ill-tempered encounter which ended with a 2-1 win for the Cobblers: English and McCulloch scoring the vital goals. Watched by referee Baker, Bournemouth captain Cunningham and Northampton's Candlin exchange pre-match handshakes, with a local supporter suitably attired for the occasion.

The Hotel End at the County Ground provides the background as goalkeeper Jack Ansell clears during a practice session. Following the restrictions imposed after the war, few ground improvements had been made when this photograph was taken. With no roof covering at the Hotel End, spectator comforts were sparse, especially when accommodating a large crowd.

Players and officials assemble before embarking on another FA Cup match in early 1950. From left to right, back row: A. Garrett, W. Barron, J. Ansell, B. Collins, M. Candlin, R. Dennison (manager), D. Smith, J. English, T. Smalley, G. Hughes, J. Jennings (trainer), E.C. Hawtin (director), A. Mitchell, T. McCoy. In front: E. Murphy, A. McCulloch, A. Dixon, P. Hutton (director).

Candlin, followed by McCoy and Dixon, leads his team back to the field for the second half of the fifth round FA Cup match at Derby County's Baseball Ground in February 1950. Derby won an exciting match 4-2, with Dixon scoring both of Northampton's goals.

Adam McCulloch challenges Derby's Townsend for possession on a very muddy pitch, in front of a crowd of 38,063.

Jack Ansell and Maurice Candlin break from training at the County Ground. The Cobblers' goalkeeper holds the old-style leather football, with prominent lacing, which was so much heavier in wet conditions than today's lighter version.

9. In consideration of the observance by the said player of the terms, provisions and conditions of this Agreement, the said...... Bertram Cheney ....on behalf of the Club hereby agrees that the said Club shall pay to the said Player the sum of £............*11*............ per week from ....1st August 1950........ to ....5th May 1951............ and £............*10*............ per week from ....6th May 1951........ to........ 31st July 1951

10. This Agreement (subject to the Rules of The Football Association) shall cease and determine on .... 31st July 1951 .... unless the same shall have been previously determined in accordance with the provisions hereinbefore set forth.

Fill in any other provisions required.

Bonuses - £2 win and £1 draw when playing in 1st Team.
£1 win and 10/- draw other matches.

£1 extra weekly wage when playing in 1st. team.

As Witness the hands of the said parties the day and year first aforesaid

Signed by the said........ Bertram Cheney .... and .... Maurice Hall Candlin ....

In the presence of

(Signature) *E. Hall.*

(Occupation) *Retired.*

(Address) *19 Lime Avenue. Northampton.*

Maurice H. Candlin. (Player).

(Secretary).

A copy of Maurice Candlin's contract from August 1950 to July 1951.

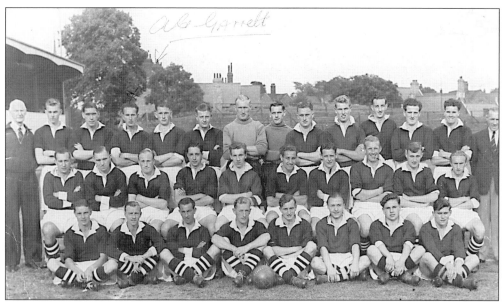

Northampton Town, 1950/51. From left to right, back row: M. Newman (assistant trainer), A. Woollard, E. Duckhouse, A. Garrett, B. Collins, M. Candlin, J. Ansell, N. Freeman, G. Hughes, J. Soloman, J. Croy, J. Docherty, A. McCulloch, J. Jennings (trainer). Middle row: W. Coley, T. Smalley, J. Southam, D. Adams, A. Jeffrey, J. Smith, J. Davie, J. Briscoe, K. Maxwell, T. Fowler. Front row: A. Mitchell, A. Dixon, E. Murphy, D. Smith, J. English, A. Hargrave, T. Smith, G. Burn. This season saw the team finish in twenty-first position, but the League performances were overshadowed by a fourth round FA Cup match at Arsenal. Although he did not achieve a first team place, Alwyn Hargrave later became Mayor of Northampton.

A happy bunch of Northampton players leave for another away fixture. From left to right: K. Maxwell, M. Candlin, A. McCulloch, E. Murphy, T. McCoy, R. King, W. Coley, J. Ansell, E.C. Hawtin (director).

In April 1951 a joint benefit match took place for David Smith (left) and Tom Smalley, with local referee Norman Hillier in charge. Both players retired at the end of the 1950/51 season.

The draw for the fourth round of the FA Cup gave Northampton Town a match with First Division Arsenal at Highbury and a day to remember for the club's supporters. On 27 January 1951 an estimated 15,000 fans left the town and county to witness the occasion. There was plenty of vocal support on the day as these excited fans showed before kick-off time.

Arsenal's Peter Goring (left) watches a shot scrape just past the post, anxiously viewed by Northampton's defenders: Hughes, Smalley, Duckhouse, Ansell and Southam. Duckhouse later became injured and spent the rest of the match on the wing.

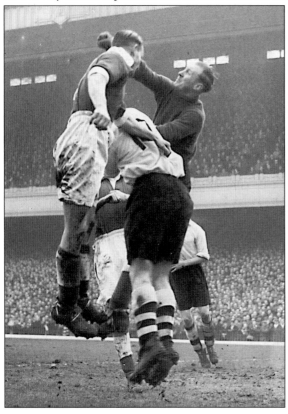

Jim Southam and Jack Ansell combine to thwart another Arsenal attack.

The first Arsenal goal, scored by grounded Reg Lewis, watched with dismay by Ansell, Candlin and Smalley. The attendance at the match was 72,408, just short of the all-time record figure for Highbury. Arsenal eventually ran out winners by 3-2, with both Northampton goals being scored by Jack English.

Jack Ansell from Bletchley first played for the Cobblers in the 1947/48 season. He stayed for five years before joining Headington United (later Oxford United) and helping his new club to the championship of the Southern League in 1952/53.

Manager Bob Dennison's team for 1951/52. From left to right, back row: B. Collins, M. Candlin, I. Feehan, E. Duckhouse, J. Wilson, G. Hughes. Front row: J. English, J. Payne, A. McCulloch, F. Ramscar, T. Fowler. Scoring 93 goals in the League, the team finished in eighth position.

Birmingham City's Ted Duckhouse signed for the Cobblers in August 1950, lending experience to the defence for two seasons. Having made 68 League appearances he transferred to Rushden Town, staying for four years until returning to the West Midlands.

The first home match of 1951/52 had an evening kick-off, with Bristol City as the visitors. The captains, Candlin of Northampton and Beasley of Bristol City, toss the coin for choice of ends. Bristol City won the match 2-1. Ramscar was the Northampton scorer in front of a crowd of over 14,000.

The Cobblers entertained a team from Luxembourg in 1951, which was designated 'Festival of Britain Year'. Owing to the County Ground being in use for cricket, the match was played at Franklins Gardens – it was a rare occurrence for such an event to be staged on the rugby ground. Players of both teams line up in front of the main stand.

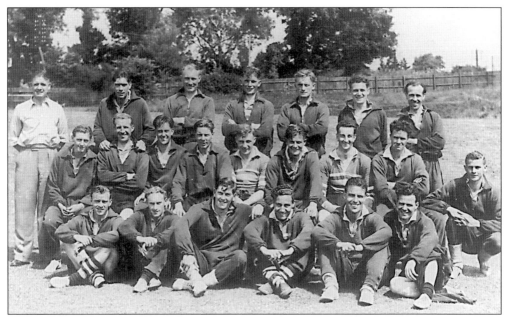

Tracksuits are the order of the day for a training session at the Trueform Sports Ground on Kettering Road, Northampton, in 1951. From left to right, back row: Hanford (assistant trainer), Duckhouse, Ansell, Collins, Hughes, Davie, Ramscar. Middle row: Raynes, Briscoe, Bowen (then on Arsenal's staff), Mitchell, Maxwell, Candlin, Croy, McCulloch. Front row: Dixon, Fowler, Feehan, J. Smith, Connell, O'Donnell, Woollard. This sports field was proposed as a site for a new stadium. However, objections from local residents prevented any developments.

The Cobblers defend in numbers in front of the crowded Abington Avenue side of the County Ground. Davie (far left), Ansell, Duckhouse and Candlin are the players involved.

ADAM
McCULLOCH
(NORTHAMPTON)

RON
PATTERSON
(Northampton)

Three of manager Bob Dennison's signings. Adam McCulloch (above left), who joined from Third Lanark in 1949, made 89 League appearances and scored 36 goals before leaving for Shrewsbury Town in 1952. Ron Patterson (above right) came from Middlesbrough in 1952 and settled in at the left-back position. By the time he moved on to Rothwell Town in 1962 he had completed over 300 League and cup appearances for the club. Fred Ramscar (right) had previously served Wolves, Queens Park Rangers and Preston North End before transferring to the Cobblers in the summer of 1951. He soon formed a left wing partnership with Tom Fowler to the delight of local supporters. He scored over 50 goals in 139 League appearances before finishing his career with Millwall in 1954/55. During his time at the County Ground he became an experienced taker of penalty kicks.

FRED
RAMSCAR
(NORTHAMPTON T.)

The Combined League XI which played Northampton Town in April 1952. The match was in aid of the joint benefit for Tom Fowler and Gwyn Hughes. From left to right, back row: W. Nicholson (Tottenham Hotspur), G. Lowrie (Coventry City), S. Owen (Luton Town), I. Feehan (Northampton Town), L. Jones (Luton Town), C. Withers (Tottenham Hotspur). Front row: A. Mitchell (Luton Town), T. Harmer (Tottenham Hotspur), G. Hughes (Northampton Town), E. Baily (Tottenham Hotspur), N. Lockhart (Coventry City). Albert Mitchell was an ex-Northampton Town player.

Thirty of the Northampton Town players for the 1952/53 season face the camera with the new roof covering at the Hotel End of the County Ground in position. From left to right, back row: J. Jennings (trainer), McLain, Hillyard, Candlin, Patterson, Connell, Adams, Feehan, Croy, Wood, Collins, G. Hughes, Dodgin, Baxter. Middle row: Wilson, Davie, English, Raynes, Mulgrew, R. Dennison (manager), Ramscar, French, J. Smith. Front row: Pinchbeck, Edelston, E. Hughes, Fowler, Hearn, O'Donnell, Payne, Briscoe, Staroscik. The team played some splendid attacking football, finishing third in Division Three (South) and scoring a record 109 goals. The forward line of English, Edelston, O'Donnell, Ramscar and Fowler each reached double figures in the goalscoring charts. Altogether only twenty players were called upon during the season. Fowler, Patterson, Southam and Wood were ever present, with English, O'Donnell and Ramscar only absent on one occasion each.

The FA Cup in 1952/53 resulted in an away fixture at Hendon in the first round. A 0-0 draw brought a midweek replay at the County Ground, which the Cobblers won 2-0 with Fowler and Ramscar scoring. This picture shows Jack English and Willie O'Donnell challenging the Hendon goalkeeper. Unfortunately, FA Cup progress was halted with a 2-0 defeat at Swindon in the following round.

Jack English scored a record 135 League goals in a career spanning 301 matches between 1947/48 and 1959/60.

Some interesting personalities appeared at the County Ground for the benefit match arranged for David Smith and Tom Smalley. From left to right: Eddie Bates (Southampton), Alf Ramsey (Tottenham Hotspur), Bill Nicholson (Tottenham Hotspur), Tommy Briggs (Coventry City), David Smith, Tom Smalley, Ben Collins (all Northampton Town), Jim Wilson (Luton Town), Norman Lockhart (Coventry City), Ken Chisholm (Coventry City), Fred Ramscar (Preston North End), Alf Wood (Coventry City). Wilson, Ramscar and Wood later joined the Cobblers.

Maurice Marston transferred from Sunderland to Northampton Town in 1953 and stayed four seasons. He finished his playing career at nearby Kettering Town.

In 1954 a managerial change became necessary when Bob Dennison stepped up to take charge of Middlesbrough. He is shown here (second from right) being congratulated by his successor, David Smith.

Left: David Smith watches Peter Pickering sign for the Cobblers in August 1955. Pickering had been playing for Kettering Town, after service with York City and Chelsea. An experienced goalkeeper, he made 86 League appearances, later emigrating to South Africa during the 1957/58 season. *Right:* For the 1954/55 season there was a growing need to replace the veteran Alf Wood in goal and George Webber was signed from Torquay United. However, he could not command a regular place and left after just one season.

Not only was Peter Pickering a splendid footballer, he was also a very useful cricketer. Owing to injury problems, he was called upon to play for Northamptonshire at Old Trafford against Lancashire in 1953. His scores of 22 and 37 were to play a major part in a one-wicket victory for his side. It was his only appearance in first-class cricket.

The 1955/56 season saw the Cobblers finish in a mid-table position, a disappointment to supporters after winning the first seven matches of the season. From left to right, back row: Eddie Smith, Jack English, Maurice Marston, Peter Pickering, Ron Patterson, Ray Yeoman. Front row: Jack Smith, Ron Newman, Ben Collins, William Dawson, Tom Fowler.

The full playing staff line up in front of the Spion Kop before commencement of the 1956/57 season. From left to right, back row: Draper, Hancocks, Marston, Elvy, Pickering, Gale, Leek, Payne (assistant trainer), Canning, Collins, Claypole, Poole. Front row: Patterson, English, Mills, Woan, Woodburn, Pryde, D. Smith (manager), Yeoman, Dutton, J. Smith, Fowler, R. Williams, Morrow.

A sunny September afternoon welcomes Maurice Marston as he leads Northampton Town onto the field for a match with Coventry City. He is closely followed by Peter Pickering and Colin Gale. The result was a 4-0 victory for the home team, with Draper and Morrow netting two goals each. The attendance was 15,291.

The 1956/57 season saw the Cobblers end up in a mid-table position in the League for a third year running. From left to right, back row: M. Marston, G. Coleman, R. Yeoman, P. Pickering, C. Gale, J. Smith, J. Jennings (trainer). Front row: J. English, R. Mills, R. Draper, A. Woan, T. Fowler. There was no joy in the FA Cup, with a 2-0 defeat at Southampton in the first round. Signed from Norwich City, Alan Woan proved to be a tremendous asset, scoring 68 League goals in 119 matches over a period of four seasons. He later served Crystal Palace and Aldershot.

Jack Smith (6) and goalkeeper Peter Pickering clear the Northampton lines during a 1-0 defeat at Queens Park Rangers in the 1956/57 campaign.

Another rearguard action, this time at Watford, sees Marston (3) saving on the line. The other Northampton players, Pickering, J. Smith and Coleman (2), watch with concern. Watford took full points with a 2-1 win.

This goalmouth scramble at Exeter resulted in Pickering collecting the ball, with Gale (5) and Marston (second from right) covering the opposing forwards. The match took place in February 1957.

Ipswich Town were champions of the Third Division (South) in 1956/57, losing only two matches at Portman Road. One of these was suffered at the hands of the Cobblers, with the only goal of the game being scored by centre forward Sid Asher. The photograph shows Pickering clearing from an Ipswich forward, with Marston (far left) and Gale in attendance.

Changes were afoot for the 1957/58 season, with the top half of the Third Division (South) helping to form the new Third Division of the Football League and the remainder being placed in the Fourth Division. A final position of thirteenth ensured the latter for the Cobblers. From left to right, back row: Ramscar (coach), Gale, Claypole, Pickering, Elvy, Green, Collins, Patterson. Middle row: Yeoman, Mills, English, Hawkings, D. Smith (manager), Leek, Woan, J. Smith. Front row: Curtis, Bright, Hall, Tebbutt, Fowler, Henson, M. Robinson.

Manager David Smith discusses tactics with his players before an FA Cup match at the County Ground against Newport County. From left to right, back row: J. Jennings (trainer), M. Robinson, J. Payne (assistant trainer), R. Corbett, P. Pickering, A. Woan. Front row: B. Hawkings, C. Gale, R. Peacock, T. Robinson, K. Leek, R. Tebbutt. The result was a 3-0 win for the Cobblers and interest in the FA Cup was a compensation in 1957/58.

A scene from the reserve match with Southampton in November 1957, with the result being an emphatic 5-1 victory for the Cobblers. The picture captures Pickering about to gather the ball, flanked by Breakwell (far left), Hadlumg (4) and Coleman (2), with plenty of spare space on the terrace in front of the main stand.

A gas fire provides some comfort for Ron Patterson, Bobby Tebbutt, Ken Leek and Roly Mills as they listen for Northampton Town's opponents in the third round of the FA Cup in 1957/58. The draw was to bring First Division Arsenal to the County Ground.

For the Cobblers, 4 January 1958 was an0 historic day. In front of a crowd of 21,344 the club achieved a famous victory by 3-1. Receipts totalled £2,700, a tremendous financial boost for a lower division outfit. From left to right, back row: David Smith (manager), Ray Yeoman, Ben Collins, Reg Elvy, Colin Gale, Ron Patterson, Roly Mills, Jack Jennings (trainer). Front row: Jack English, Bobby Tebbutt, Barry Hawkings, Ken Leek, Tommy Fowler.

The programme for the Arsenal match. The Arsenal team included three names that were later to be synonymous with the Cobblers. The Arsenal half-back line was: Cliff Holton, Bill Dodgin and David Bowen.

Bobby Tebbutt, Jack Smith, Barry Hawkings and Tommy Fowler have an early start for the fourth round FA Cup match at Liverpool. Wintry conditions did not prevent the match being played but, despite a fighting display, the Cobblers were beaten 3-1. Apart from the FA Cup, the League position became a concern and even wins of 7-2 against Millwall and 9-0 against Exeter City could not prevent the club entering the Fourth Division in 1958/59.

JACK JENNINGS TESTIMONIAL MATCH

"COBBLERS" v.

Combined League XI.

TUESDAY, APRIL 13th, 1954

to be held at

COUNTY GROUND, NORTHAMPTON

By kind permission of
Northampton Town Football Club Ltd.

SOUVENIR PROGRAMME — THREEPENCE

A caricature of Jack Jennings, which was drawn for his testimonial match, portrays the speed with which he ran onto the field to attend to injured players, always urged on by the crowd. He commenced his football career with Wigan Borough in 1924 and later played for Cardiff City, Middlesbrough, Preston North End and Bradford Park Avenue. He must have been close to international honours as he was chosen to tour Canada with the FA team in 1931. A wartime guest for the Cobblers, he later became trainer and was considered an expert on sports injuries. In addition to his football duties he was called upon to assist the British Olympic team and spent the 1965/66 winter with the MCC cricket team that toured Australia and New Zealand. Throughout his service at the County Ground he was always on hand to help local sportsmen and women and many tributes were forthcoming when he died in 1997.

Five

The Swinging Sixties

The appointment of David Bowen as player-manager in July 1959 was to herald a new outlook for Northampton Town. He had been at the County Ground as a youngster before signing for Arsenal and during his career he was capped 19 times for Wales. After the 1959/60 season he retired from playing to concentrate upon management, with spectacular results.

The inauguration of floodlighting at the County Ground took place on 10 October 1960, with Arsenal as the visitors.

Peterborough United's election to the Football League in 1960 helped to inspire Northampton Town's efforts and at the end of the 1960/61 season promotion had been assured. The 90 goals scored were the result of some splendid attacking football. From left to right, back row: Colin Gale, Ralph Phillips, Tony Claypole, Tony Brewer, Derek Leck, Mick Wright. Front row: Bela Olah, Mike Deakin, Roly Mills, Tom Fowler, Barry Cooke. At the beginning of the following season Mick Wright left the County Ground to return to his East Anglian roots, eventually making over 1,000 appearances for non-League King's Lynn.

The 1960/61 players assemble in front of the team coach prior to departure for an away fixture. From left to right: J. Jennings (trainer), R. Phillips, M. Deakin, D. Bowen (manager), T. Claypole, B. Olah, M. Wright, C. Gale, T. Fowler, D. Leck, L. Brown. B. Cooke is standing with the driver on the coach step. On this occassion the goalkeeper, T. Brewer, appears to have missed the photo call! Amateur international Laurie Brown had joined the club earlier in the season, having previously played for Bishop Auckland and Darlington. His ability became noted at higher levels and at the the end of the seaosn he was transferred to Arsenal – much to the chagrin of the County Ground fraternity. Later in his career he played for Tottenham Hotspur, Norwich City and Bradford Park Avenue.

David Bowen was never afraid to change his team in the constant search for a successful side and this 1961/62 team was an example of his drive and dedication. From left to right, back row: J. Jennings (trainer), W.R. Osborne (secretary), R. Edwards, D. Leck, T. Branston, N. Coe, T. Foley, C. Brodie, A. Woollard, T. Robson, R. Mills, D. Bowen (manager), J. Payne (assistant trainer). Front row: M. Everitt, D. Woods, C. Holton, J. Reid, B. Lines.

Cliff Holton (seen here in Arsenal colours) was possibly one of the finest players ever to wear a claret and white shirt. He made his debut at Crystal Palace in September 1961, and immediately announced his presence by scoring a hat-trick in a 4-1 win.

This cartoon from the *Northampton Chronicle & Echo* records Cliff Holton's feat of breaking Ted Bowen's goals tally for a League season. He possessed a tremendous shot from either foot, was capable of withstanding strong challenges and was good in the air. He scored 50 League goals in only 62 appearances and his 36 goals in 1961/62 gave him a second scoring record to add to his previous feat of notching 42 in 1959/60 for Watford.

Derek Leck, signed from Millwall in 1958, was to play a prominent part in the team's rise from the Fourth Division to the First Division in the early 1960s. Capable of playing in defence or attack, he became an essential part of David Bowen's team selection. He later finished his career with Brighton.

Barry Lines from Bletchley signed for the Cobblers at the age of eighteen, taking over the outside left position from Tommy Fowler. He made his debut in November 1960 in a 3-3 draw with Hartlepools United at the County Ground.

David Bowen maintained his links with Arsenal, making one of his signings Mike Everitt. Originally playing in the forward line, he later became a reliable full-back. He first appeared at the County Ground in front of 21,000 spectators when Peterborough United defeated the Cobblers 3-0 in February 1961.

After making 154 appearances for Exeter City, Theo Foley signed for the Cobblers in 1961. He soon became a regular in the first team and was later a partner with Mike Everitt in the full-back position. This photograph shows him in his capacity as club captain. He was also capped for the Republic of Ireland.

Northampton Town, the 1962/63 Division Three champions. From left to right, back row: D. Bowen (manager), J. Jennings (trainer), A. Ashworth, D. Leck, F. Large, C. Brodie, T. Branston, J. Kurila, V. Cockcroft, W.R. Osborne (secretary), J. Payne (assistant trainer). Front row: M. Everitt, W. Hails, R. Smith, T. Foley, B. Lines, J. Reid, R. Mills. This momentous season produced 109 goals, a total which equalled the 1952/53 tally – a remarkable accomplishment considering the long break in mid-season due to severe weather conditions. The final match against Hull City at the County Ground did not take place until 24 May. One of David Bowen's most astute signings was Frank Large, who scored 18 goals in 20 matches despite only arriving in mid-season. This was the ever-dependable Large's first of three periods of service with the club.

Three of the formidable forward line are seen in action during this match – which seems to have attracted a good crowd judging by the lack of standing room on the terraces. The Northampton players, from left to right, are: John Reid, Ray Smith and Barry Lines.

Another important transfer was that of Billy Hails from local rivals, Peterborough United. His experience proved invaluable, especially when in tandem on the right wing with his former Peterborough colleague, Ray Smith.

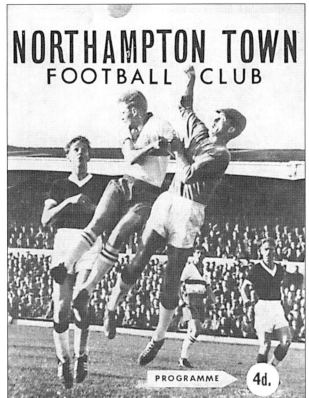

Despite the success on the field, the small programme produced for the season hardly did the team justice. This programme, which portrays Branston, Brodie and Mills in action, was issued for the match with Southend United, when a hat-trick from Frank Large helped to give the Cobblers a 5-3 victory.

The 1963/64 season saw the Cobblers finish in a comfortable eleventh position in the Second Division. This cartoon shows some of the determined players who helped the team establish itself in higher circles. The 2-0 win over Southampton was revenge for the earlier 3-1 defeat at The Dell and a tribute to the defence that did not concede a goal to a team that scored 100 goals in the season.

Goalkeeper Norman Coe was another Arsenal import who joined the Cobblers in 1960. He stayed for six seasons, leaving in 1966 to join King's Lynn.

Tommy Robson, a youngster from Gateshead, signed for the Cobblers in 1961. He was a no-nonsense type of winger who gave over 70 wholehearted appearances for the team, scoring 20 League goals. He moved on to Chelsea in 1965, later playing for Newcastle and Peterborough United. A prolonged stay at Peterborough brought him a record number of 440 appearances and a further 42 as substitute.

The Northampton Town team that won promotion from the Second Division in 1964/65, with an unbeaten home record in 21 games. From left to right, back row: W.R. Osborne (secretary), Graham Carr, Joe Kiernan, Derek Leck, Bryan Harvey, Terry Branston, Bobby Brown, Don Martin, Mike Everitt, J. Payne (trainer). Front row: Harry Walden, Theo Foley, D. Bowen (manager), Bobby Hunt, Tommy Robson.

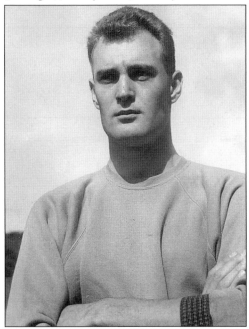

Bryan Harvey had an outstanding season in 1964/65, his goalkeeping being of the highest standard. Saving no fewer than seven penalties, he added to the reputation of one of the best defences in the club's history.

A cartoon that summed up the 1964/65 season for the team and supporters.

Bobby Brown, a former England amateur international, joined the Cobblers in 1963/64, having previously played for Fulham and Watford. He established himself in the team midway through the 1964/65 promotion season and scored 13 goals in 20 matches, making the number nine shirt his own. He was the leading scorer with 9 goals in the club's only season in the First Division and later assisted Cardiff City.

Northampton Town's staff assemble for their memorable debut in the Football League's First Division in 1965/66. From left to right, back row: Foley, Carr, Everitt, Bates, Kurila, Branston, Walton. Middle row: J. Payne (trainer), Lines, Best, Leck, Barron, Linnell, Harvey, Mackin, Cockcroft, Kiernan, R. Mills (assistant trainer). Middle row: Walden, Hall, Livesey, Hunt, D. Bowen (manager), Brown, Martin, Etheridge, Robson. Front row: Howe, Fagan, Price, Bamforth. A good start to the season was essential, but no win until the fourteenth match against West Ham United always left the team with much work to do. However, the results improved until 23 April 1966, a day always remembered by the 24,523 record crowd that crammed into the County Ground to witness the 4-2 defeat at the hands of relegation-haunted Fulham. After this a return to the Second Division became inevitable. The average attendance for home matches was 18,633, with a minimum admission fee of four shillings. Joe Kiernan was the only player to play in all 42 League games.

Daventry-born Roly Mills signed for Northampton Town in 1951 and remained with the club for thirty-nine years. He served as a player (305 League appearances), assistant trainer and, later, as a member of the commercial staff. During his playing career he was selected for every position, with the exception of goalkeeper and centre half. When he retired at the end of the 1963/64 season he had scored 30 League goals. Mills represented England at Youth level.

The teams for the second home match, against Manchester United. A crowd of 21,245 enthusiasts witnessed Bobby Hunt net a late equaliser in a 1-1 draw. Somehow, the small programme format did not appear to reflect the visit of such a magical name in the soccer world.

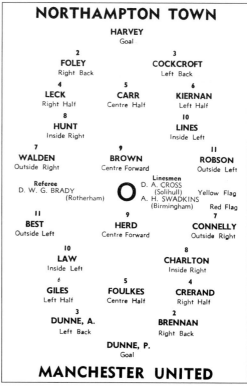

NORTHAMPTON TOWN

HARVEY
Goal

2
FOLEY
Right Back

3
COCKCROFT
Left Back

4
LECK
Right Half

5
CARR
Centre Half

6
KIERNAN
Left Half

8
HUNT
Inside Right

10
LINES
Inside Left

7
WALDEN
Outside Right

9
BROWN
Centre Forward

11
ROBSON
Outside Left

Referee
D. W. G. BRADY
(Rotherham)

O

Linesmen
D. A. CROSS
(Solihull)   Yellow Flag
A. H. SWADKINS
(Birmingham)   Red Flag

11
BEST
Outside Left

9
HERD
Centre Forward

7
CONNELLY
Outside Right

10
LAW
Inside Left

8
CHARLTON
Inside Right

6
GILES
Left Half

5
FOULKES
Centre Half

4
CRERAND
Right Half

3
DUNNE, A.
Left Back

2
BRENNAN
Right Back

DUNNE, P.
Goal

MANCHESTER UNITED

A *Chronicle and Echo* cartoon preserving the memory of a 3-1 victory over Newcastle United.

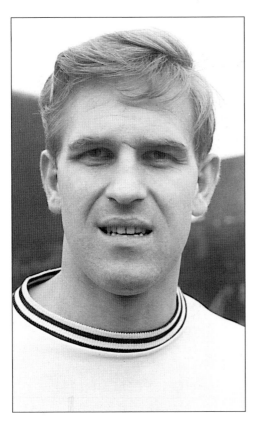

The lack of goals from the forward line was a concern for David Bowen and, being in charge of the Welsh international squad, he signed Graham Moore, a skilful player from Manchester United. Moore made an immediate impact and added to his collection of Welsh caps. After 53 appearances and 10 goals, Moore moved to Charlton Athletic, finally completing his career at Doncaster Rovers.

Joe Broadfoot, an experienced winger with both Millwall and Ipswich, joined the staff at the County Ground in November 1965 but, despite scoring in his second match against Blackpool, failed to settle in the team.

Manager David Bowen introduced nineteen-year-old Jim Hall into his team in March 1964. Born in Northampton, Hall showed much promise in the forward line and was considered good enough to appear in 15 matches in the First Division. He later transferred to local rivals Peterborough United, playing in 298 matches and scoring 120 goals before returning to the Cobblers in 1975. His career also included a short spell with Cambridge United. In his early years Hall represented England at youth international level.

Graham Carr made his debut in the 1962/63 season and remained on the Northampton staff until 1967/68, when he joined York City. Later in his career affiliations with non-League football gave him management experience, which led to a return to the County Ground and the building of a promotion team in 1986/87.

The Northampton Town team of 1968/69 face the camera at the Hotel End of the County Ground. At the end of the season there was little to cheer about with the club resigned to relegation to the Fourth Division. The long journey to the First Division and back had now been completed. From left to right, back row: Ron Flowers (player-manager), John Roberts, John Clarke, John Mackin, Roger Barron, John Byrne, Dennis Brown, Frank Rankmore, Peter Gordon (trainer/coach). Front row: John Fairbrother, Brian Faulkes, Eric Weaver, Joe Kiernan, Graham Felton, Clive Walker, Barry Lines, Tommy Knox, Ray Fairfax.

Joe Kiernan (6) and mud-covered goalkeeper Roger Barron prepare to defend the Northampton goal against Bristol Rovers at Eastville during the late sixties.

Six

The Seventies
Managerial Changes 7 Successes 1

Frank Large (left) and Phil Neal take to the field for a lower division encounter in the early seventies. Apart from the 1975/76 season, there was not a lot for Northampton Town fans to cheer about in this decade. Even the FA Cup saw four defeats by non-League teams: Hereford United (twice), Leatherhead and Enfield.

Ex-Arsenal player, Bill Dodgin, was appointed as manager in 1973 and gave the club much-needed impetus. His team of 1975/76 won promotion to the Third Division, finishing as runners-up to Lincoln City. The team won 29 out of the 46-match programme and remained unbeaten at home. To much surprise Dodgin resigned during the summer of 1976, but returned for another spell of management in October 1980. (Bob Thomas/Popperfoto)

Phil Neal's last appearance for the Cobblers was on 5 October 1974. The match was against Rotherham United at Millmoor and for the last twenty minutes he replaced goalkeeper Alan Starling, who had been injured. The match ended in a 3-1 win for the visitors and Neal was able to sign for Liverpool, a career move which brought him 50 caps for England and 8 League Championship medals. From 1968 to retirement in 1989 he made 718 League appearances: 186 with Northampton, 455 at Liverpool and 77 with Bolton Wanderers. (Bob Thomas/Popperfoto)

The promotion team of 1975/76. From left to right: Steve Phillips, Barry Tucker, Billy Best, Andy McGowan, Derrick Christie, Paul Stratford, John Farrington, Don Martin, David Carlton, Jeff Parton, Jim Hall, Alan Starling, John Gregory, Stuart Robertson. (Bob Thomas/Popperfoto)

Jim Hall in action at Vicarage Road against Watford as the 1975/76 promotion push enters the final stages. The Cobblers won this vital match 1-0, Hall scoring the winning goal. He finished the campaign with 21 League goals. (Bob Thomas/Popperfoto)

Paul Stratford, a Northampton-born player, had a highly promising season in 1975/76 and was being noticed by the higher division clubs. Sadly, injures plagued him and within two years he had been forced to retire from the game (Bob Thomas/Popperfoto)

Friends on and off the field, Barry Tucker (left) and John Gregory celebrate at Valley Parade having beaten Bradford City 2-1, a win that signified promotion to Division Three for 1976/77. A poor start in 1976/77 saw the champagne go flat and after one season the team returned to the Fourth Division. Barry Tucker later transferred to Brentford, returning to the County Ground in 1982 for two more seasons. John Gregory took another route, signing for Aston Villa and being capped for England. Top division management eventually followed for Gregory, a position now held at Villa Park. (Bob Thomas/Popperfoto)

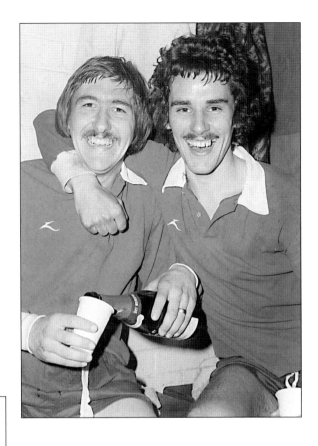

JOHN CLARKE

BENEFIT MATCH

by Robert Thomas

NORTHAMPTON TOWN

v

LEICESTER CITY

MONDAY, 12th APRIL, 1976 · K.O. 7.30 p.m.

OFFICIAL PROGRAMME   PRICE 10p

Another local boy, John Clarke, played over 250 League and cup games for the Cobblers. Making his debut against Portsmouth in October 1966, his career was cut short following two cartilage operations. After ten seasons he was awarded a benefit match, with Leicester City as the visitors.

Action from the second round match of the Football League Cup in 1977/78. Stuart Robertson (right) tussles with an Ipswich Town forward. The Suffolk club won 5-1. (Bob Thomas/Popperfoto)

The end of the Portman Road encounter and Stuart Robertson congratulates Eric Gates of Ipswich on a comprehensive victory. (Bob Thomas/Popperfoto)

The jubilation on the faces of Stuart Robertson (right) and Paul Stratford (centre) indicates that the Cobblers have registered a goal. (Bob Thomas/Popperfoto)

Northampton
Town
Football Club

FOOTBALL LEAGUE DIVISION FOUR

NORTHAMPTON TOWN

v

NEWPORT COUNTY

SATURDAY, 5th NOVEMBER, 1977 - K.O. 3 p.m.

Cobblers
Players
A-Z
Guide

David Liddle

David Liddle Made his debut this season in the Football League Cup first round at Southend. Had a run of 11 games in the first team at centre back. Came to the Club as a striker from Bedford as an apprentice, but was switched to defence last season.

OFFICIAL PROGRAMME   PRICE 15p

The programme format in use for the 1977/78 season. The team finished in tenth position in the Fourth Division, the highly rated George Reilly finishing as top scorer with 21 goals. It is interesting to note that the previous game, away to Rochdale, was only witnessed by 1,198 spectators. Newport County won the advertised match by 4-2.

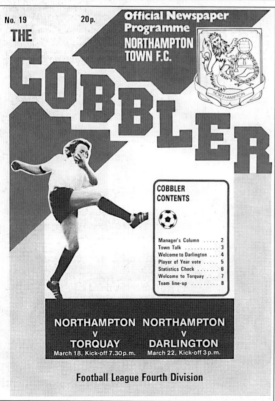

Northampton Town, 1978/79. From left to right, back row: Derek Christie, Paul Saunders, Peter Mead, Keith Williams. Middle row: Mike Keen (manager), Jim McNichol, Neil Cordice, Carl Jayes, Andrew Poole, Steve Bryant, John Farrington, Clive Walker (coach). Front row: George Reilly, David Liddie, Alan Woollett, Stuart Robertson, Kim Wassell, Ricky Walker. A disappointing season found the club only avoiding re-election by two points with the result that Mike Keen was replaced by Clive Walker as manager.

The designs of the match programmes were constantly changing, with the 1979/80 edition taking on a miniature newspaper appearance. This particular issue covered two matches: Torquay were beaten 3-0 and Darlington 2-0. Under Clive Walker's management the club ended in thirteenth position in the Fourth Division.

Seven

Renaissance Under Graham Carr

Graham Carr's team for 1985/86. From left to right, back row: Carr (manager), Clarke (youth team manager), Schiavi, Dawes, Gleasure, Reed, Hill, Nohilly, Walker (assistant manager). Front row: Lewis, Curtis, Benjamin, Barnes, Morley, Mundee, Brown, Mann, Cavener. Eighth position in the final table gave a hint of better times to come.

The Fourth Division champions of 1986/87. A wonderful season saw the team score 103 goals and record 30 wins in the 46-match programme. The basis of Carr's team-building revolved around knowledge of the non-League scene. He recruited Morley and Hill from Nuneaton Borough, Wilcox from Frickley and Gilbert from Boston United. From left to right, back row: G. Donegal, M. Bushell, R. Coy, M. Schiavi, R. Hill. Middle row: C. Walker (assistant manager), I. Benjamin, G. Reed, P. Gleasure, R. Wilcox, K. McPherson, D. Casey (physiotherapist). Front row: P. Curtis, D. Gilbert, T. Morley, G. Carr (manager), P. Chard, W. Donald, A. Mann.

Trevor Morley (left) having scored against Peterborough United in the local derby at the County Ground and Richard Hill repeats the exercise in the 1-1 draw away to Exeter City.

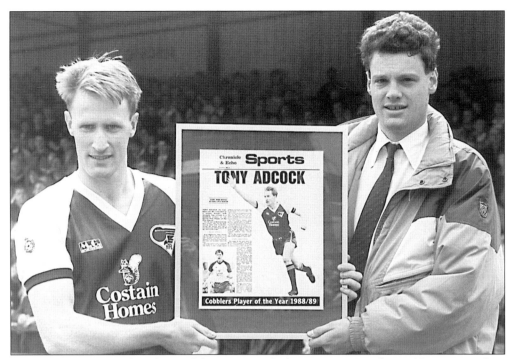

Tony Adcock receives his Player of the Year award after scoring 17 goals in 46 League matches. His goals were vital in a season where the Cobblers escaped relegation by a narrow margin over Southend United.

The sun was shining for this pre-season team photograph session of 1989/90, but a few months later the Cobblers were to face relegation back to the Fourth Division. From left to right, back row: M. Singleton, W. Donald, W. Williams, D. Thomas, D. Collins, P. Gleasure, P. Culpin, S. Berry, B. Sandeman, M. Tarry. Middle row: C. Walker (assistant manager), P. Wilson, T. Adcock, R. Wilcox, D. Johnson, G. Donegal, K. McPherson, S. Brown, T. Quow, B. Knight (reserve team manager), D. Casey (physiotherapist). Manager Graham Carr is seated on the far left of the front row together with the club's directors.

If the League performances proved disheartening, the FA Cup gave some crumbs of comfort. The opening round drew the Cobblers with Kettering Town at Rockingham Road on 18 November 1989. The result was a 1-0 win for the County Ground team. This picture shows Russell Wilcox in action against the Kettering Town goalkeeper, Kevin Shoemake.

Another action photograph from the Kettering match shows Darren Collins (9) outnumbered by the home defence. In the background Keith McPherson awaits developments. The match drew 6,100 spectators.

Eight

The Nervous Nineties

The headline news in May 1990 revealed that Graham Carr had tendered his resignation as manager, coupled with the problems that had been festering at board level. More important to club followers was the team's relegation to Division Four.

Not only did the Cobblers say goodbye to Graham Carr in 1990, the club also recorded the death of Harry Warden. This devoted employee commenced duties as a gateman in 1920, later becoming the club's general factotum, a position he retained until just before his death. The FA acknowledged his services with an award in 1985.

Theo Foley returned to the County Ground as manager following Graham Carr's departure. With his playing days over, he had turned his attention to the managerial side of football. His appointment, together with Joe Kiernan as his assistant, brought back memories of the club's glory days in the sixties. Financial difficulties, however, restricted his plans to build a promotion team and two years later he left the club.

In April 1991, Michael McRitchie took over as club chairman. His optimism could not hide the desperate financial plight or the inescapable fact that the County Ground was rated as one of the worst grounds in the Football League. His troubles were soon to mount.

PUBLIC MEETING

THE FUTURE OF NORTHAMPTON TOWN FOOTBALL CLUB

Date : Thursday 2nd January
Venue: Exeter Rooms , Exeter Place, Kettering Rd
Kick-Off :7.30pm

Team Line-ups (Those invited):-

Michael McRitchie, Theo Foley, Trevor Quow (PFA Rep), The Players, Former players, The Leaders of the Local Political Parties, Press, Radio and TV

Tonight's Referee (Chairing the Meeting): Brian Lomax

ALSO INVITED --- YOU!

Meeting organised by WALOC

A simple printed notice announcing a meeting in January 1992. History will probably record this event as being one of the most important factors in the fortunes of Northampton Town Football Club. A large attendance sparked off ideas that helped to bring the club back from the brink of extinction.

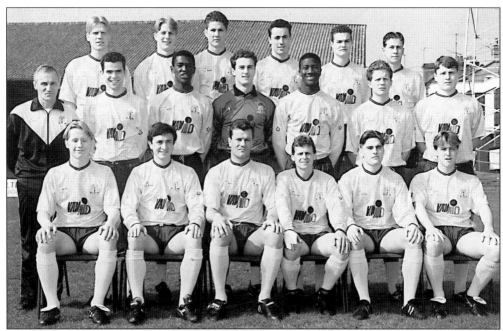

The dark days of 1992 heralded the appointment of a firm of administrators, which in turn resulted in ten players being released from the staff. The remaining players face the camera in March of that year. From left to right, back row: Simon Underwood, Lee Colkin, Martin Aldridge, Jimmy Benton, Mark Parsons, Graham Wright. Middle row: Denis Casey (physiotherapist), Danny Kiernan, Steve Brown, Barry Richardson, Terry Angus, James Waring, Craig Adams. Front row: Jason Burnham, Phil Chard (player-manager), Steve Terry, Stuart Beavon, Mickey Bell, Sean Parker.

Fans gather for the final home match of the 1993/94 season against Chester City, a game that was originally billed as the last appearance of the Cobblers at the County Ground. The late completion of the new stadium at Sixfields delayed the final appearance at Abington Avenue until October 1994 when Mansfield Town were the visitors.

Originally signed on loan from York City, Ray Warburton became a dominating influence in defence. This picture, taken at the Chester City fixture, shows him in action with an opposing inside forward. A crowd of 6,432 packed into the County Ground to witness the Cobblers win 1-0. Despite this victory the club finished in bottom position in Division Three and were saved from relegation to the Conference only by Kidderminster Harriers not meeting ground requirements.

Mickey Bell in action against Chester City. His goal in a 2-1 win against Carlisle United in September 1994 remains a historic event, being the last goal scored by a Northampton Town player in a League game at the County Ground.

The winter sunshine shows through the remaining girders and roof as the Hotel End is demolished at the County Ground in January 1995.

The remnants of the main stand are reduced to rubble and Abington Avenue residents would soon be able to overlook the cricket section of the County Ground. This view was soon to be lost with the development of the Indoor Cricket Centre.

A turnstile shows signs of wear at the Hotel End. How many people had passed through this entrance over the years?

Out with the old and on with the new. This youngster watches with anticipation as the new stadium at Sixfields nears completion in 1994.

The splendid new stadium at Sixfields heralds a new chapter in the history of Northampton Town Football Club.

The first visitors at Sixfields were Barnet on 15 October 1994. A crowd of 7,461 were in attendance to see Martin Aldridge score the first Northampton Town goal at the stadium. Supporters will long remember his somersault as he celebrated with his colleagues. Sadly, he was to lose his life in a car accident in early 2000.

Experienced both as a player and at management level, Ian Atkins was appointed to the managerial chair in January 1995. Before coming to Northampton he had played in the higher divisions of the Football League, appearing with Birmingham City, Sunderland and Everton. He had also served Colchester United, Cambridge United and Doncaster Rovers as manager. He was to make a big impact on the club's fortunes.

Neil Grayson, signed in 1994 from non-League Boston United, soon became a favourite with supporters with his 100 per cent endeavour. An important member of the team that reached the 1997 play-off at Wembley, he will always be remembered for recording a hat-trick in four minutes against Hartlepool earlier in the 1996/97 season.

Goalkeeper Andy Woodman, an early signing by manager Ian Atkins, came to the Cobblers from Exeter City in March 1995.

Manager Ian Atkins built his team up with some experienced players, Ian Sampson from Sunderland being a key figure in his plans. Now with over 250 League appearances, he has more than justified his signing.

Ian Clarkson, a free transfer signing from Stoke City, gave some sterling performances for the Cobblers before an injury curtailed his career. He later joined non-League Kidderminster Harriers and was a member of their team that won promotion from the Nationwide Conference in 1999/2000.

After several seasons with his local club, Birmingham City, John Frain came to Sixfields in 1997. He will always be remembered for scoring from the free kick in the final moments of the Wembley play-off against Swansea City, a goal that ensured the club's promotion to the Second Division in May 1997.

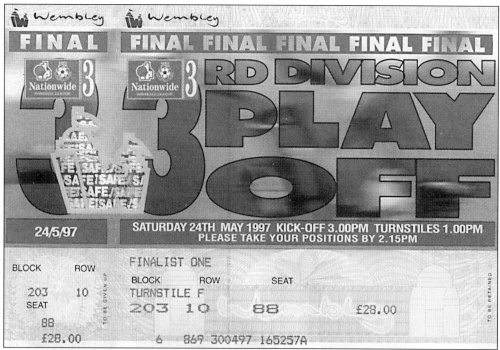

A souvenir of the club's first ever appearance at Wembley.

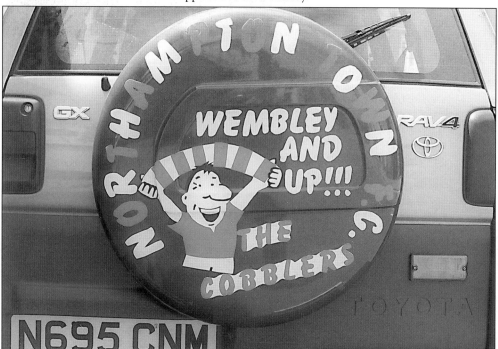

An example of the enthusiasm of the Northampton Town support for the match with Swansea City. A total of 46,804 attended the match. A year later 62,988 witnessed another Wembley appearance for the Cobblers against Grimsby Town, although a 1-0 defeat ended further promotion ambitions.

Skipper Ray Warburton lifts the Maunsell Cup in 1997 after his team had defeated Kettering Town. He later joined Rushden and Diamonds in their quest to attain Football League status.

Capped 42 times for Northern Ireland, Kevin Wilson came to the Cobblers from Walsall having spent many seasons in the higher leagues. After making a few League appearances he succeeded Ian Atkins in the manager's chair in 1999/2000 and led the Cobblers to an automatic promotion place in Division Three.

The celebrations in the dressing room at Torquay after a 2-1 win confirmed the Cobblers would be playing in Division Two in 2000/2001. (Pete Norton)